Larder Limericks

With best wishes
Oliver Preston

Also published by
Robson Books
Liquid Limericks
Titillation for tipplers

Larder Limericks

Five-Liners for Foodies

Pictures by Oliver Preston
Script by Alistair Sampson

ROBSON BOOKS

For Camilla, my beloved wife of thirty-seven years.

With lips so red and eyes so blue,
And teeth so pearly white.
You're more than patriotic,
You're a very pleasant sight.
AS

For Amber
OP

First published in Great Britain in 2004 by Robson Books,
The Chrysalis Building, Bramley Road, London, W10 6SP

An imprint of **Chrysalis** Books Group plc

Copyright © 2004 Alistair Sampson and Oliver Preston

British Library Cataloguing in Publication Data
A catalogue record for this title is available from the British Library.

ISBN 1 86105 806 3

Original artwork from this book is available to buy at
www.oliverpreston.com

Printed in Spain

Foreword

I've known Alistair Sampson since the early 80s when he would pop in for a spot of lunch at my restaurant Menage à Trois in Beauchamp Place, Knightsbridge. His journey was but a short distance from his antique shop.

As a young chef, I often felt like a rebuked schoolboy, as his voice, while confident, appeared to growl like a wolf moving in for the kill.... Little did I know that beneath this smooth-suited antique dealer's fearsome charm lay a wit of gargantuan proportions, so sit down with a nice, chilled glass of Chablis and gorge yourself on *Larder Limericks*. Alistair Sampson and Oliver Preston have delivered a superb dish for you to savour.

Alistair's simple but engaging wit comes over so well, complimented by Oliver's strong observations in the form of his illustrations. A deft use of the English language and Oliver's pencil is just as sharp.

And there I am to be immortalised in limerick, surely this is to have arrived in life!

A wonderful tome – I doubt if there is one person who would not have a loud chuckle at the limericks this book has on offer.

Antony Worrall Thompson

Saint Antony

Now I never, not ever,
  would quarrel
With a fellow like Antony
  Worrall
Thompson, who's fine;
Friendly and benign.
Not even acidic like sorrel.

PREFACE
The Glutton's Prayer

Give me this day my daily bread –
Or maybe chocolate cake instead.
Or caviar or Stilton cheese.
Lord, give me anything you please.

I am allergic, may I say
To tripe and onions, curds and whey.
Do please forgive me, I forgot
You are omniscient – know the lot.

But, to remind you, Irish Stew
Is one thing I adore – don't you?
Scotch Broth, Welsh Rarebit, both are right
For my voracious appetite.

When I'm in France, do not forget
To give me daily my baguette.
Also, when I go abroad
Save me from temptation, Lord.

May I on each foreign hol
Remember my cholesterol.
Save me, I beg you, Father, please
From high-cal Swiss patisseries.

Spare me, oh Lord, all that's en crème
Do that then hallow'd be thy name.
Lest Lord I should become a bore
I trespass on your time no more –

Save, may I earn such daily bread
As leaves me adequately fed?

Worth It

There once was a dish name of Fleur
Who was anything but Cordon Bleu.
Tho' her food was inedible
She was blissfully beddable –
Eat out, then sleep in? I concur.

Bang Goes the Meringue!

I was suddenly flung to my knees.
I said to the waiter 'Oh please,
'What's the commotion?
'Why the explosion?'
He replied 'It's a Bombe Surprise'.

OLIVER PRESTON

Sang-Froid

Nat suddenly noticed a rat in
His wife's Macaroni au Gratin.
He said, 'Tell you what's best
'Carry on with the rest
'While I go out and summon the cat in.'

Cool Cat

Last Saturday while at the footie
Sven decided to eat his jam butty.
Just imagine his eyes
And his look of surprise
When out of it jumped his cat Sooty.

Lettuce Eat

Here's to the ladies who lunch
That giggly, gossipy bunch.
Disposable nappies.
Disposable chappies.
Divorce, if it comes
to the crunch.

Green About the Gills

Some think AA Gill is a pill
When he goes for the kill with his quill.
But at least he is fond
Of a bird called 'The Blonde'.
So maybe there's good in him still.

OLIVER PRESTON

Minute Steak

'I know that you serve your steak rare.
'But is this really all you can spare?
'Is it rare as all that?
'This would not feed a cat.'
'Sir, this is between you – to share.'

A Good Egg

She's a good egg, my girlfriend, twice nightly
She and I do a once over lightly.
Before breakfast a cup
Then it's sunny-side up.
'You organic?' I ask her politely.

Doggerel

'No dogs and no smoking? You joke!
'Why, your owner's a mean-minded bloke.
'He can keep his hotel
''Tis the hostel from hell.
As it happens, our dog doesn't smoke.'

'Did I hear you correctly: "No doggies?"
'And doubtless – it follows – no moggies?
'So we can't stay a spell
'At your splendid hotel
''Till our poor little mutt's popped his cloggies.'

'No dogs in hotel,' said Chi-Ming
When he rang from his inn in Beijing.
'What, no more Roast Poodle
'Or Labrador Strudel?
'Please cancel our booking, old thing.'

Keeping Up Standards

I in my DJ, Anne in her orange and gold
We stand at the portals waiting to be received.
'Jolly to see you – come in out of the cold.'
If one did not know one could not have believed

That four hours before she stood in Sainsbury's
In her jeans and her sheepskin and queued like the rest,
Queued with the gardener and the daily and all
Those humble folk who do not have a crest.

Now radiant and soignée she glides through her hall,
Passing the flowers arranged by her own hand.
As was her hair – alone she has done it all –
Making the house and herself look positively grand.

She has cooked like a queen. She and her husband serve;
Wispily weaving their way in the lamplight.
He has laid the table, polished the glasses and
cleaned the silver.
How polished indeed they both are – and how bright.

When we have all gone, he will roll up his sleeves
And clear, and turn to his wife and say,
'Why the bloody hell do we half kill ourselves
Carrying on in this silly, pretentious way?'

A Sense of Proportion

Whenever you fish for whitebait
Take care to use the right bait.
As whitebait are uncommonly small
And make the humble sprat look tall,
The right bait is a light bait.

Dinner's on You

Let us for once push out the boat.
To Hell with prix fixe and table d'hote.
Let us not care a fart.
Let us go à la carte –
Do a runner – but send a thank-you note.

Ready, Steady, Cook!

I'd like to get my paws on
That dish Nigella Lawson.
I'd close the kitchen door and lock it,
Lay her on a bed of rocket,
Then pour some chocolate sauce on.

Yummy Tummy

As Margot grew bigger and bigger,
She developed a fine fuller figure.
She would gorge on cream cakes
Now she has what it takes
For voluptuous
lovers to dig her.

Cornish Rhapsody

Mr Stein is just fine on his wine,
While his fish is quite simply divine.
So rich mums and dads go
Each summer to Padstow
Stand in line just to dine with Rick Stein.

In the End It's Just Money

A fish-loving diner called Sid
Ate a mountainous helping of squid.
Then he fainted away,
And unconscious he lay.
The squid had cost two hundred quid!

The Loyal Toast

'Unaccustomed as I am to public squeaking'
(Said the mouse as they passed round the cheese),
'Let us rise and drink a toast
'To our very charming host
'And his Pont L'Evecs, his Boursins and his Bries.'

'I give you, brother mice, the open larder
'Coupled with Her Majesty the Queen.
'Death to that imposter
'Imported Double Gloucester
'You really never know where it has been.'

'Therefore fellow gastronomic rodents –
'I ask you now to charge your glasses, please
'And to drink with one accord
'To our host's next trip abroad
'To Normandy – to buy a little cheese.'

Dear Old Mother

Hol is topping. Mum goes shopping
By lunch time she is always dropping.

'Let's give all our chums a buffet,'
I suggested. Mum said, 'Stuff it!'

In the pool we're wildly sploshing;
Mum is busy with the washing.

While we in the pool are playing
Mother does the table laying.

At English papers we are looking
While dear Mater does the cooking.

Pretty hot beside the Aga:
Really, she does deserve a lager.

How we love to go self-cater.
We all dig it, don't we, Mater?

OLIVER PRESTON

La Belle France Gastronomique

Oh Côte d'Azur! Such happy days!
Soupe de poisson; Bouillabaisse!
Coquilles St Jacques
Then sadly it's back
To fish and chips and rainy days.

And Nut Cutlets to You, Too

Said a New Yorker beanpole, 'I feel
'That no-one should ever eat veal.
'Even hungry Hungarians
'Should become vegetarians
'Who really needs a square meal?'

PRESTON

OLIVER PRESTON

Cooking Above Oneself

A pretentious young creature from Chard
Was given to trying too hard.
Her rose-petal sambal
Was not a good gamble –
Not to speak of her
Crab rémoulade.

Jolly Japes

A young ray of sunshine called Hank
Would pop to his host's septic tank.
And then with a whoop
Produce huge bowls of soup.
To be frank, as a prank, it just stank.

Death Wish

Michael Winner is coming to dinner.
We really must help him get thinner.
So all that he'll get is
A small leaf of lettuce,
And maybe a glass of retsina.

Saturation Point

No more I've stomach
for the fight.
Diminished is my appetite.
Rejoin the scene
Nouvelle cuisine.
One lettuce leaf!
Oh, rare delight!

PRESTON

Not Our Night

Little did Amanda ever dream of the disgrace
She was to bring upon me on the eighteenth of July;
The night we went for dinner with the Brands in Eaton Place –
A night I shall remember with remorse until I die.

We arrived at half-past seven and discovered far too late
(We had lost the invitation and forgotten what it said.)
We should have been in evening dress and should have
come at eight.
But Lady Brand was charming and so beautifully bred.

I asked for a martini and made some little joke
About martini cocktails always setting me on fire;
I later learnt her country pad had just gone up in smoke.
Lady Brand said nothing so I went on to admire

Their Picassos and their Monets and their four Toulouse-Lautrecs.
And their Degas and their Turner; then I saw Sir Robert wince
It transpired they'd been burgled of most of their effects
And filled the empty spaces with these rather tatty prints.

By my third or fourth martini the others had appeared;
'Where's your charming husband?' I enquired of Mrs Gorst.
Then I mumbled little nothings and I stroked my absent beard –
As it suddenly came back to me – they'd only just divorced.

We all went into dinner where I quickly broke a chair –
Lady Brand was super and said, 'Perfectly all right
'Although it's smashed to ribbons I'm sure it will repair –
'They are so fearfully fragile, these painted Hepplewhite.'

Amanda started twitching so I lit a cigarette,
Thinking I could wait until the port for my cigar.
'I wonder,' asked Sir Robert, 'If you'd mind not smoking yet?'
Then I dropped some apple crumble down Mrs Brimstone's bra.

Every time I took a sip or two I saw Amanda frown.
I think she had concluded I'd had just about enough.
Maybe she was worried I was going to let her down;
While I was quietly certain I was made of sterner stuff.

I complimented Lady Brand upon her choice of meat.
'What lovely lamb,' I rashly cried. She told me it was beef.
I drooled about the burgundy and found it was Lafite.
Amanda led the girls out with a look of deep relief.

I myself was in no hurry – I had gone before I came.
I settled down to chatter over Cockburn's '24.
I could hardly get a word in, but I finally found fame
As I drowned their conversation with an
intermittent snore.

Later: when we joined the ladies, Amanda said a pain
Had suddenly afflicted her and she was feeling sick.
And off we went and since that night we've not been back again.
And all because Amanda dropped that monumental brick.

I mean, when one has eaten such a simply lovely meal
And one says to all and sundry that one is not feeling well,
It really was insensitive. What must one's hostess feel?
When I got Amanda home I really gave her hell.

Fifteen

Now Jamie's a pukka good lad,
And deserves the success that he's had.
Without blinding and effs
He turns kids into chefs.
Yes, he's really not doing too bad!

Coming Out of One's Shell

They do say that oysters are amorous.
My darling, you're looking quite glamorous.
Twenty-four number twos
And a fair bit of booze
Will doubtless, in due course, enamour us.

A Day Out

We like to go alfresco
When it's remotely fine,
With pre-sliced bread from Tesco
And screwtop Spanish wine.

Of course you won't be sick, Dick
Just remember, take your pill.
We much prefer a picnic
To a café and a bill.

Make sure you pack the trannie
And piles of plastic plates.
The rug can go on Grannie –
So can Cyril's skates.

We like to be away by
Ten forty-five or so.
Eyes open for a lay-by
Where the diesels gently blow

Hot exhaust fumes on the flora
And small particles of dust.
Coca-Cola, Laura?
And who would like the crust?

Maybe dear old Pa might
Now he's got his teeth.

There's raspberry jam or Marmite.
No more Kit Kat, Keith.

We never leave much litter –
Just lengths of polythene
And empty cans of bitter
So people know we've been.

Rising Early

Ever since we've been wed
We've had breakfast in bed.
My Cynthia usually
Kicks off with muesli.
I take Viagra instead.

Talk of the Town

Jemima, a charming young trollop
Was chased but not chaste. Nether Wallop
Was her home. Said the town,
'She'll undress and go down
'For a clam, let alone for a
scallop.'

Uncle Charlie's blue eyes
used to twinkle.
He was eighty with hardly
a wrinkle.
'I am quite an old-timer,'
He said to Jemima,
'Tell me – what would you
do for a winkle?'

The Gordon Riots

The Connaught, once known for its game
Will never again be the same.
Every buffer disparages
The changes at Claridge's.
Gordon Ramsey, you're wholly to blame.

Gott in Himmel

A chef can behave like a Führer
And frequently lose his tempura.
Gordon, act like a man,
Curb your tongue if you can.
Do stop effing and blinding.
Talk purer.

An Elegant Sufficiency

Cousin Edmund would frequently say,
'I am, my dear chap, a gourmet
'Tho' of food I am fond,
'I am not a gourmand.
'I know when to call it a day.'

Expat

I'm just a fella –
A fella with a paella.
So I think I'll remain
On a plain here in Spain
And endeavour to write
a bestseller.

OLIVER PRESTON

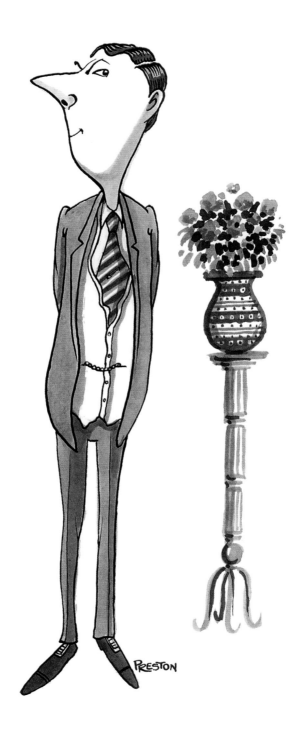

Thrilled to the Core

Maud has a 'thing' about Coxes
Though apples per se leave her cold.
It is odd, Maud's affection for Coxes –
She has had it since seven years old.

The Bramley or Russet,
She will not discuss it;
'The Pippin is rippin','
That's all she will say.

Maud gave no apples to teachers –
Nor ate one each day like the rest –
But when she stopped boarding
They found she'd been hoarding
Boxes of Coxes in chest after chest.

Had she been kissed in an orchard –
With blossoming buds on the bough?
Well, the key that unlocks
Maudie's heart is a Cox –
So that's what I'm taking her now.

Gourmet's End

'The ashes have come from Harrods
'Where should they lie, my Lord?'
'James, place them in the cool room –
'Where the caviar is stored.'

'Let her lie with the marrons glacés
'That she never could resist:
'In a wreath of Helford oysters –
'The reason that she is missed.'

'Take her from the cool room
'And place her in the Rolls
'While the vicar seeks God's blessing
'On all departed souls.'

'I regret to inform your Lordship
'There has been a slight mistake.
'Cook accidentally used her
'To decorate a cake.'

A Sad Thyme

We all have little vices.
Rosemary's was spices.
When her Basil ran out,
She just fell about
Into a mid-life crisis.

Out for a Duck

She gave my hand a squeeze
And said, 'Let's go Chinese.
'You could be in luck –
'If it's Peking Duck
'I shall do my best to please.'

BASIL

ROSEMARY

THYME

SAGE

OLIVER PRESTON

A Litany for Feathered Friends

We are in season from today.
We are the pheasants – let us pray.
From twelve-bored bores on moors preserve us,
We beseech thee; we are nervous.

Save us, we pray, from flights in crates
To France or the United States.
If we must die we should prefer
The Berkeley or the Dorchester.

Hear us, we pray, and grant us this –
God save the Queen and make them miss.
Although it's thought grouse always choose
If they must go, to go in twos,

Yet belted earls do not need braces
To crown their days in open spaces.
Please let us spy their gleaming barrels –
Let us survive for Christmas carols.

Please put water in their cartridges
And spare our little pals the partridges.
Spare us, we pray, the birds thy friends
To thank thee when the season ends.

A Friend In Need

It's so nice to have a mouse about the house
And to feel that little chaps
Will jump upon one's traps
And eat one's little scraps.
It's just grand to see a head above the bread;
And to know the open tin
Will have a mousie in
Busy at his din.
It's just fine to hear a scratch behind the hatch
And to know that not far away
There's a mousekins who'll say,
'I had Camembert today.'

Playing the Field

Though food is still my passion
In a most promiscuous fashion
Since my decree
In bed I'll be
Life's one long degustation.

No Nibble is Good Nibbles

The Scotsman said, 'Nay, not today.
'Take these amuses-gueles away
'And the amuses-bouches and the petits fours.
'Och, aye – but I am terrible poor.
'I canna pay for the canapés.'

Big Business

Indulgence in gastronomy
May not be an economy,
But a slap-up meal
Does a powerful deal
To promote a banker's bonhomie.

Plateau de Fruits de Mer

'What's in our seafood platter?'
'Monsieur what does it matter?
'There's a cockle, a clam, a piece of hake,
'Which somehow got there by mistake
'So we covered it all in batter.'

'There's a small langouste, whose left-hand nipper
'Contains a piece of half-cooked kipper.
'I tell you what's fab
'Is the well-dressed crab
'The moules are cool and the squid is chipper.'

'It comes straight from the sea, sir
'Via a short stay in our freezer
'If after you dine,
'You don't feel fine,
'We might reduce our fee, sir.'

PRESTON

Fryday

I'm a husband who does a mean fry-up.
It's so tiring I afterwards lie up,
Which assists my digestion
And ensures there's no question
Of my helping to wash up and dry up.

The Grass is Greener

'We're having a joint,' our hostess said.
To turn her down would be ill-bred.
We said, 'Why not?'
The joint was pot.
'With roast potatoes?' asked my Fred.

Spot-on

A spotty young schoolboy called Rick
Said, 'Oh Matron, I'm cut to the quick.
'My acne's improved
'But, oh Matron, it's moved.
'Have I eaten too much Spotted Dick?'

Fin de Repas

'If I'm to eat Devils on Horseback
'May I please have the horseradish sauce back?'
'That beggars belief,'
Said his host, 'It's for beef.'
'Then please may I have the last course back?'

ROAST
MASH
CHIPS
NEW

CLOSED

MR
SPUD

DAUPHINOISE
CROQUETTES
BAKED

OLIVER PRESTON

On Giving Up Potatoes

So – my affair
With the pommes de terre
Is over for a while.
Sound the Last Post
For the Sunday roast.
Say farewell with a smile
To pommes croquettes
And allumettes
And boiled and mashed and new
And frozen and tinned
And baked and skinned
And swimming in a stew.
'Tis au revoir
To Dauphinoises
And saddest of all goodbye
For many a day
To Lyonnais
And that sweet little Frite, French fry.

Pizza San Marco

Pierre White is quite often in Drones –
A joint he both eats at and owns.
His whisk's on the shelf,
Does no cooking himself,
And makes do with a series of clones.

Dish of the Day

I deeply and profoundly wish
That you would be my signature dish.
'Tis you I adore
Be my plat du jour;
For darling, I am hungryish.

Achtung Wildlife

Only huns of inordinate wealth
Can afford to shoot grouse on the twelfth.
They fire at the birdies
With Bosses and Purdeys;
Poor creatures, so bad for their health.

Run for Your Life

There once was a very wild duck
Who, before being cooked, ran amok.
Although the chef chased him
The quacker outpaced him.
Said the chef, 'He's too plucky to pluck.'

Cook Booked!

Delia keeps the lupine from the portals.
In fact, she earns a crust more than mere mortals.
She leads the good fairies
That feed the Canaries.
'My dear Norwich eat your porridge oats,' she chortles.

Horses for Courses

A fine-looking filly called Sal
When show jumping would ride her cheval.
While in France her main course
Was a nice slice of horse.
She rode 'em and ate 'em; some gal.

OLIVER PRESTON

Love's Sweet Song

Look, I tell you, sonny,
I am not being funny.
You cannot beat
As a morning treat
A roll in bed with honey.

The Gun Who...

We were at the smartest shoot.
For lunch there was boeuf en croute.
Then some arriviste
Got terribly pissed
And proceeded to shoot a coot.

Something for Afters

I said to the waiter, 'Look smart.
'This evening I feel like a tart.'
'There's my sister,' he said.
'She's a tigress in bed.
'She's called Tatin and comes à la carte.'

Champers for Campers

When Teddy goes camping, he pampers
His deeply obliged fellow campers.
He takes care to hasten
To Fortnum and Mason
Who deliver the very best hampers.

The result? Why, they never complain
Be it blowing and pouring with rain.
Each holding his toggle
Their little eyes boggle
To see the game pies and
Champagne.

Round the camp-fire they drink to,
'Our Teddy,
'May he long be possessed
of the ready.
'How kind that he brought, 'em,
'These hampers from Fortnum.'
No wonder his friends
are so steady.

Hurrah for the Virgin Sturgeon

Dear Madam,
'Tis not what the scene is,
To put lumpfish on top of your blinis.
Can't run to Beluga?
Make do with Sevruga.
We can't have you known as the meanies.

There's No Such Thing as a Freehold Lunch

An estate agent cried out,
'Forsooth,
'My profits have gone through
the roof.
'But it bugs me like hell,
'When I'm doing so well,
'That I have to eat lunch on
the hoof.'

OLIVER PRESTON

E.C. on the Eye

WANTED: A girl to cook meals
For one of the City's big wheels.
Who'll cook Crêpes Suzettes
Who won't play hard to get,
And then squeals as he feels while he deals.

How Not to Get Driven Barmy

Unless you are keen on salami
Don't join the Italian army.
Nor should you gaily
Become an Israeli
If you faint at the sight of pastrami.

Every Woman has her Price

A floosie who played hard to get
Asked a farmer to buy her Raclette.
As he wrote out the cheque
He said, 'This is on Spec –
'It is yours for a cuddle, my pet.'

Please Feel Free to Eat While We Smoke

We never light up till the port.
We really don't think that we ought.
Then we watch you all choke
As you breathe passive smoke.
Without doubt it's our favourite sport.

OLIVER PRESTON

Eat, Drink and Be Merry

The best cocktail parties are Sybil's.
About that there can be no quibbles.
It's not just the drinks
It's the way that the minx
Gives each boyfriend an earful of nibbles.

That'll Cook Your Goose!

Said the goose to the turkey, 'Remember,
'We must make ourselves scarce in November.
'As you are a turkey,
'Your future is murky –
'By twelfth night you'll be but an ember.'

Investing for the Long Term

'Let us get away from the hoi polloi,'
My uncle said, 'to the Savoy.
'We'll eat in the Grill;
'If you pay the bill,
'I'll remember you in my will – dear boy.'

Haute Price Cuisine

When I have a fit of the blues,
I eat out with one of the Rouxs.
Do I go posh,
And pick the Gavroche,
Or give Bray a whirl? Tricky to choose.

Slippery Customer

They had hardly sat down at their meal
When Ethel misplaced her smoked eel.
She cried, 'Ron, my dear Ron,
'You won't guess where it's gone.'
Said Ronald, 'Just how does it feel?'

Hail to the Clam

'As a favour,' said Dwight, 'you're allowed a
'Small bowl of my mommy's clam chowder.
'While you arrogant Brits
'May sneer at our grits
'Ma's chowder sure makes us feel prouder.'

OLIVER PRESTON

Battle Stations

'We are the stuffed peppers,' the Colonel said.
He was beautifully dressed and perfectly bred.
The waitress's smile could not have been broader –
'Mr Stuffed Pepper, what did you order?'
If looks could have killed, she'd have dropped down dead.

Deep-filled Granny

Every Friday my gran goes out shopping.
She shops all day long 'till she's dropping.
Then she comes home and eats a
Huge takeaway pizza
With every conceivable topping.

The Narrow-Minded Broad

As folk don't intrude down in Bude
I said, 'Let's go swim in the nude.
'Then we'll each eat a peach
'As we romp on the beach.'
She frowned. I said, 'Don't be a prude.'

On the one Hand...

Bless, oh Lord, the food we eat –
Fish and fowl and good red meat,
Sweetbread, suckling pig and veal,
Calves' liver, foie gras, baby seal,

Jugged hare, tame rabbit, kangaroo,
Koala bears from Sydney Zoo,
Baby monkeys from Uganda,
Chinese meals of giant panda.

Why devour our fellow creatures?
Why eat anything with features?
Let us, Lord, not be barbarian
Let us all turn vegetarian.

To save us, Lord, You paid the price.
Must turkeys make this sacrifice?

And On the Other...

The pigs, the cows, the sheep, oh Lord,
You put upon this earth,
Did You hope they'd be ignored
And given a wide berth?

When You fed the multitude,
Was it not Your wish –
Did You, oh Lord, not say that You'd –
Be glad if they ate fish?

So when the tiger hunts its prey
And fish eat other fishes,
Must we assume that such as they
Ignore their Maker's wishes?